⟫ TRIBUTE ⟪

*A guide to Seattle's public parks and buildings
named for black people,
with brief biographical sketches*

by
Mary T. Henry

drawings by
Marilyn H. Henry

STATICE PRESS

1997

STATICE PRESS • PO BOX 22198 • SEATTLE, WA 98122-0198

Printed in Canada
Designed by Krishna Gopa

Published by Peanut Butter Publishing
Pier 55, 1101 Alaskan Way, Suite 301
Seattle, WA 98101-2982
206-748-0345 • e-mail: pnutpub@aol.com
http://www.pbpublishing.com
Denver, Colorado • Scottsdale, Arizona
Portland, Oregon • Vancouver, BC

LCCCN: 97-69-095
ISBN: 0-89716-762-7

♻ Printed on recycled paper

SUPPORTED BY THE KING COUNTY LANDMARKS AND HERITAGE
COMMISSION HOTEL MOTEL TAX REVENUES

This book is dedicated to the memory of
E. June Smith, 1900–1982,
a leader in Seattle's civil rights movement.

❧ ACKNOWLEDGEMENTS ❧

IT WAS MY PLEASURE, during the research for this book, to meet many gracious and extremely helpful people. They include: Scott Cline, City Archivist; Janet Evans, Rosemary Wills and Jennifer Cargal of the Department of Parks and Recreation; Seattle Public Librarians at the Downtown Library and at Douglass-Truth; Eleanor Towes, Seattle School Archivist; Andrea Welch of Carolyn Downs Family Health Center; Linda Vassar of Odessa Brown Children's Clinic; Richard Edwards of the Meredith Mathews East Madison YMCA; Candace Coe of Epiphany School; Cornelius Bradley, Manager of Gideon-Mathews Gardens; Austrid Martin, Librarian at Garfield High School; and Danie Eagleton, Project Director of Alvirita Little Center for Girls.

I am very grateful to those who lent assistance to the project by granting interviews and by providing source material: Ginny Larkins, Emilee Capps, Lillian Gideon, Elmer Dixon, Luther Carr, Roger Soder, Attorney Christopher Mathews, Attorney Lavida Mathews, Dr. Meredith Mathews, John Cannon, Judge Charles Johnson, Feralyn Carter, DeCharlene Williams, Alvirita Little, Isadora Downs, Douglass Barnett, Vivian Lee, Toby Burton, Herman McKinney and Mr. and Mrs. Oscar Braxton.

Many thanks go to Esther Mumford, Olaf Kvamme and to my son Neil Henry who read the manuscript and offered valuable criticism and encouragement. I am grateful to Charles Payton, Community Museum Advisor, for his wise counsel.

Lastly, I must thank my son, Bob Henry, who after the evening meals, cleared the dining room table, washed the dishes and set up the lighting for Marilyn to complete the drawings for the book.

❧ CONTENTS ❧

❧ FOREWORD ❧

T HE CITY OF SEATTLE is a city of diversity. People of different races, religions, ethnic, cultural and professional backgrounds are contributing factors to the whole. Public vistas and landmarks also tell a lot about a city's character, personality, vitality and spirit. They are set aside for public use and exist for all citizens to enjoy. Their names have special significance and add much to the local lore and history. There are 23 such public parks and buildings in Seattle named for black people.

Well before the turn of the century, African Americans made significant contributions to the character, spirit, sparkle and well-being of the City of Seattle. During World War II many blacks arrived in the Pacific Northwest and the population really began to swell. They came from all parts of the country. Some were members of the US military stationed in Seattle and others worked in the ship yards to assist with the war effort.

Inspired and equipped with their heritage of faith and hard work, they came together to build a sense of community. In spite of hostile conditions that sometimes beset them, they harnessed their energies to build homes and churches. Their children attended public schools and other institutions of higher learning. They started and became involved with local civic, social and service organizations. They became educators, writers, musicians, health care providers and social and civil rights activists.

Mary T. Henry, author of *Tribute*, a guidebook to public parks and buildings provides us with insightful and important information surrounding the lives of 22 black people for whom Seattle parks and buildings are named. Her research gives us a brief glimpse of history and the opportunity to read, be inspired, visit and learn more about the who and why of the names associated with some of Seattle's landmarks.

Norman B. Rice
Mayor, City of Seattle

❧ INTRODUCTION ❧

T HE FACE OF A CITY reflects the hopes and dreams of its people, their ideals and their heroes. Nowhere in a city is it reflected more than in the names of its landmarks. Our streets are named for early settlers and national heroes; our parks and school buildings are named for people who in some way have made a contribution to our area or our nation. Yet, in our daily rounds of the city, we cross these streets, pass parks and buildings bearing names that we take for granted, sometimes never understanding or even knowing their significance.

This guide book is intended to acquaint the reader with the public parks and buildings in Seattle named for black people and to give an identity to these individuals. Included are 23 sites named for 22 people. Most are located in the Central Area. Twelve are buildings, eight are parks, one is a playground, one is a water play area and one is a viewpoint.

All but two are either agencies of United Way or under the auspices of the City or the Seattle School District. The Carolyn Downs Family Health Center is a federally qualified clinic and a satellite of Country Doctor Clinics. The Odessa Brown Children's Clinic is a satellite of Children's Hospital.

Seven of the persons memorialized were nationally and internationally known. The remaining 15 were local citizens who made unusual contributions to the quality of life in Seattle. Whether in the arts, civil rights, health, social service, business or education, their lives made an impact on our city. The sites now honoring black people were named between 1969 and 1996.

Prior to World War II there had been two public places in Seattle named for black women. The Sojourner Truth Home, named for the abolitionist, was located at 1422 23rd Avenue. The Phyllis Wheatley YWCA, named for the Revolutionary War era poet, was at 102 21st Avenue North.

In February 1968, the voters of King County and the City of Seattle approved seven Forward Thrust bond issues and pledged $333,900,000 to the betterment of the community over a 12 year period. The Central Area of Seattle gained parks, mini-parks, a swimming pool and a playground from this commitment. The Washington State Interagency for Outdoor Recreation, Housing and Urban Development, Model Cities and Central Area Motivation Project were also partners in the purchase or development of these facilities.

The sudden increase of parks and recreation facilities prompted the Department of Parks and Recreation Board to establish a policy for naming them in 1969. It was amended in 1971, 1974 and 1985.

The Parks and Recreation Naming Committee consists of the Superintendent of Parks and Recreation, the Chairman of the Board of Park Commissioners and the Chairman of the City Operations Committee of the City Council. Suggestions for names are solicited from organizations, individuals and the media. The Committee recommends a name to the Superintendent who will designate that name for a park or a recreation facility. A name once bestowed is permanent.

The Seattle School District can change the name of the school upon significant neighborhood support. Suggested names for new schools are requested from the community. Names that provide inspiration for young people receive highest consideration. The School Board makes the final decision regarding a school name. Community or neighborhood support can also influence the City in changing the name of a City owned building.

It is hoped that as you walk or drive past these landmarks, you will pause and consider the lives of the people for whom they are named and the reasons behind the community's choice of the names. It is also hoped that you will share this guide with young people and take them to these places to be inspired by the dedication of those memorialized.

Numbers in parentheses refer to references used. (8, 111, 117)

❧ Al Larkins Park ❧

*U*NTIL 1979 THIS 0.7 ACRE in the Madrona Community was known as the 34th and Pike Mini Park. The land was bought by Forward Thrust funds in 1970 and developed in 1975. It is located on the northern edge of a small business area on 34th Avenue giving neighboring residents and strolling pedestrians a pleasant block of greenery.

A concrete path winds through the contoured grounds lush with pine, fir, cedar and maple trees and where benches are placed in strategic locations for intimate conversations or quiet meditation. This is a favorite place for volleyball and football or for tossing frisbees. For the past few years the worshippers at St. Therese, Madrona Presbyterian and Church of the Epiphany have gathered at the park on Palm Sunday for the blessing of palms.

On January 9, 1979, this peaceful little park was named for Alvin Larkins upon recommendation by the Madrona Community Council and approval by the Superintendent of Parks and Recreation.

A bronze identification plaque with a portrait of Mr. Larkins was placed in the park on October 14, 1989, by the Madrona Community Council.

Bus 2 to East Pike

Bus 3 to East Union. Walk north one block.

(19, 44,61,75,121)

ALVIN LARKINS
July 15, 1924 – May 18, 1977

SO MANY PEOPLE from all segments of the city packed Madrona Presbyterian Church on the day of Alvin Larkins' memorial service in 1977 that a friend later said, "I had no idea Al was so well known." Though small in stature, Al Larkins had boasted an enormous capacity for friendship and it was expressed through music and teaching. He had possessed an open, caring manner which attracted all kinds of people, old and young, white and black and made him an effective and trusted teacher.

Born in Baltimore, Mr. Larkins did not arrive in Seattle until 1943 when, as a Naval enlistee, he was stationed at Sand Point Naval Base. He was part of the Jive Bombers, a group of professional jazz musicians there. After World War II he remained in the area working in Bremerton with the Welfare Department and with the Veterans Administration in Seattle. In 1952 he enrolled at the University of Washington for a degree in education. His career as a teacher began in the Seattle Public Schools four years later when he taught social studies and band at Wilson Junior High School. For the last nine years of his life he taught social studies at Franklin High School, working closely with the Black Student Union. From 1966 to 1968 he also worked with the University of Washington Upward Bound Program.

Mr. Larkins, a brilliant bass fiddler and tuba player, was a longtime member of Seattle's Rainy City Jazz Band and an original performer in the Seattle World's Fair Marching Band. He was well known for playing bass fiddle at theaters and concerts throughout the area. The first Bumbershoot Jazz Festival featured him and his brother Ellis.

Mr. Larkins devoted much of his time to the Madrona community where he lived since 1949. He directed the choir for 15 years at the Madrona Presbyterian Church, served as co-president of the Madrona School PTA and was a familiar figure playing the bass fiddle at the Madrona Mayfair and for the Christmas ships at Madrona Beach.

On the night of May 18, 1977, after another day spent teaching his beloved students at Franklin and at Echo Glen, Mr. Larkins died suddenly of a heart attack. Mr. Larkins had requested that his body be given to the University of Washington for medical research. It was an act of generosity and concern typical of the teacher's life. Two years later, when it came time to pick a suitable name to grace the small, tranquil park at 34th Avenue and East Pike Street, the Madrona Community Council quickly decided on Al Larkins.

(75, 84, 93)

⊰❖ THE ALVIRITA LITTLE CENTER FOR GIRLS ❖⊱

HE CENTER FOR GIRLS INCORPORATED of YWCA, formerly Girls Club of Puget Sound, was named in 1991 for its founder. In 1996 Girls Club Incorporated of Puget Sound united with the YWCA. The Center is located at 708 Martin Luther King, Jr. Way and houses the administrative center as well as the activities center.

Alvirita Little spearheaded the fund raising to purchase the property from the Urban League in 1971 by appealing to churches and writing proposals to Boeing Good Neighbors, Junior League, Weyerhauser and the Medina Foundation. She became its first executive director.

The two-story building has been remodeled and extended since its dedication in 1972 as the only facility bought with community contributions and dedicated to girls. Today, it houses a teen center, classrooms, gymnasium, outside deck and concrete play area. A colorful mural by Jackie Day of Mrs. Little and groups of girls is on a wall in the gymnasium.

The Center serves girls ranging in age from 6 to 18 in before and after school activities during the school year and in all day activities during the summer. Current programs include hands on scientific discovery, substance abuse prevention, pregnancy prevention and informal education that empowers girls to live and succeed in an inequitable world.

A Center in West Seattle was opened in 1983 in a facility donated by Seattle Housing Authority. The Girls Incorporated of YWCA is part of a national network of over 300 affiliates in 135 cities that serve more than a quarter million girls. It is a member of United Way.

Bus 3 to Martin Luther King, Jr. Way. Walk north a few feet.

(90,94)

ALVIRITA LITTLE
b. May 25, 1913

ALVIRITA LITTLE was born on a farm in Spring, Texas, the eighth of nine children in the Charlie Wells family. Her grandfather came to the United States as a slave from the area now called Liberia. He labored for a group of German Methodist Christians and after emancipation they gave him farm land on which his descendants lived and worked.

As a farm girl Mrs. Little walked miles to school. After completing high school she married Arthur Booker and had five children. Her second marriage was to Frank Little, a career U. S. Army soldier who retired in 1964 after 30 years of service. While stationed in Japan, Mrs. Little received her B.A. Degree at St. Frances Catholic School in Tokyo. The family moved to Seattle in 1951 and she promptly took part in community activities.

She has maintained a continuing interest in the Foundation for International Understanding Through Students, having hosted 217 young people from 46 foreign countries. She has also contributed her time and energy to the Seattle Urban League, United Way, Atlantic Street Center and the United Methodist Church. But it was her association with the Seattle Council of Churches that sparked a dynamic and lasting legacy.

In 1969 a black mother approached the group with the plea from her daughter that for girls, unlike for boys, there was nothing to do and there were no places to go. This prompted Mrs. Little to orga-nize activities, beginning with a picnic at Salt Water State Park for seven girls. Eventually 35 girls, volunteer drivers and community churches were involved in cooking, sewing and swimming classes on Saturdays. Two years later the group had an organized board, served 85 girls and became affiliated with the Girls Clubs of America. Mrs. Little served as the first Executive Director of the Girls Club of Puget Sound and through her efforts its present home on Martin Luther King, Jr. Way was purchased.

A trim, gracious woman, Mrs. Little speaks with a lingering south-ern accent and wears her hair pulled tightly back into a chignon. When asked how she managed to be involved in so many commu-nity activities, she smiled serenely and said, "Through the help of God and a good husband."

(94)

⋘ Dr. Blanche Lavizzo Park ⋙

ORMING A PATHWAY between South Jackson Street and East Yesler Way, this narrow, fairly secluded park is bordered on the east and west by apartments and private homes. It is graced with many trees and unusual amenities.

When entering the park from 22nd Avenue South and East Yesler Way one walks down a series of steps which form an amphitheater used in summer for free concerts and other community gatherings. A large grassy area boasts picnic tables and grills. A picnic shelter, complete with fireplace, is shielded by a line of poplar trees. The interior of the shelter was once brightened by a colorful mural titled "New Millennium Jazz; A Jackson Street Tradition Lives On" and produced by the 1995 art students of Seattle Central Community College.

On the walkway which extends to South Jackson one will pass a long shelter house and a bricked open area with benches. Here in the shade of oak trees visitors can rest on their walk and enjoy the aromas wafting from nearby bakeries.

This 1.953 acre park was known as the Yesler Atlantic Pedestrian Pathway until October 1991, when it was renamed for the first medical director of the Odessa Brown Children's Clinic. It was funded by Urban Renewal and designed in 1977 by the firm of Sakuma, James and Petersen. Initially developed by the Department of Community Development, the jurisdiction of the park has been transferred to the Seattle Department of Parks and Recreation.

Bus 27 to 22nd Avenue South. Walk south to the steps.

Bus 14 to 22nd Avenue South

(19,115)

⋘ Dr. Blanche Lavizzo Water Play Area ⋙

*T*HIS WATER PLAY AREA at the Edwin T. Pratt Park is located at 20th Avenue South and South Washington Street. It was dedicated on July 11, 1995. The area features African-themed images and designs including two water columns and three animal sculptures which delight children with their water sprays. The team of artists which produced the images and designs included Marita Dingus, Monad Elohim, Roosevelt Lewis, Eric Salisbury, Daniel Menter and Samaj.

The park was the inspiration of a group of people closely associated with the Odessa Brown Children's Clinic who wanted to honor its founding medical director with a play area for children. The group included Dr. Abe Bergman, Toby Burton, Liz Thomas and Linda Vassar. They felt that the Dr. Blanche Lavizzo Park, one block away, was too secluded for such an activity. It is fitting that this memorial be placed in the Pratt Park because of the close friendship between the Pratt and Lavizzo families.

A bronze plaque with an image of Dr. Lavizzo, identifying text and a poem by Alice Walker, is on site.

Bus 27 to 20th Avenue South. Walk south to South Washington Street.

(31, 16, 39, 46, 83)

DR. BLANCHE SELLERS LAVIZZO
July 11, 1925 – August 28, 1984

D R. BLANCHE SELLERS LAVIZZO was a mother, wife and pediatrician when she arrived in Seattle in July 1956. She and her surgeon husband, Dr. Philip Lavizzo, had left medical practices in New Orleans, Louisiana in order to pursue their careers in the Northwest.

Until 1970, when the Odessa Brown Clinic opened its doors at 2017 East Spruce and she became its first medical director, Dr. Lavizzo had been in the private practice of pediatrics. She cared for children in her office and made house calls to them at night. Her presence was always a source of comfort to concerned parents.

In her position as medical director of the clinic she became the mainstay of health care for children in the Central Area and it was she who gave the clinic its motto "Quality care with dignity." "She placed her mark on the way the clinic was run, from the way the staff answered the phone to seeing that the chairs in the waiting room were comfortable," commented a colleague.

Born July 11, 1925, in Atlanta, Georgia, she was a friend and schoolmate of Dr. Martin Luther King, Jr. Her father was the owner of one of Atlanta's largest black funeral homes. She graduated from Spelman College in 1946 and Meharry Medical College in 1950. In

1975, she received a Masters in Public Health from the University of Washington.

Dr. Lavizzo was small in stature and carried herself with great dignity. She had a splendid sense of humor, recognized by those who knew her well. She was an avid duplicate bridge player and an opera lover. An active force in the black community, she served on the board of the Girls Club of Puget Sound and as president of the Seattle Chapter of Links, Inc. She contributed her time to many other community organizations including the Seattle Urban League, United Way of King County and numerous health organizations.

In 1972, Dr. Philip Lavizzo died and Dr. Blanche was left a widow with four children. During that year her closely cropped hair began to turn completely white. In the following years, she balanced her roles as single mother and physician with courage and grace. She became suddenly ill in July 1984, was hospitalized at Providence Hospital, and died on August 28, 1984. The mass of Christian burial was held at Immaculate Conception Church and interment was at Holyrood Cemetery.

(37, 51, 52)

❧ CAROLYN DOWNS ❧
FAMILY MEDICAL CENTER

O N DECEMBER 1, 1969, the Black Panther Party, in an effort
to address the health needs of black citizens in the Central
Area, opened the Sidney Miller Free Medical Clinic. The
clinic was named for the young Black Panther who was shot and killed
by a grocery store clerk in West Seattle after an attempted robbery.

The first location of the clinic was in a rented house at 169 19th
Avenue which also served as headquarters of the Seattle Black Pan-
ther Party. Its later locations were at 18th Avenue and East Union
Street and at 20th Avenue and East Spruce Street.

By 1975, the clinic closed because of dwindling funds and the loss
of medical volunteers. Through a neighborhood consortium of
health agencies, federal funding was applied for and granted. In 1979
a building at 1422 34th Avenue was purchased and the clinic
reopened as the Carolyn Downs Family Medical Center in honor of

the young Black Panther who succumbed to cancer in 1978.

In 1994 the medical center moved to 2101 East Yesler Way in the redesigned and enlarged Odessa Brown Children's Clinic. The building is now known as the Central Area Health Center housing the family medical center, the children's clinic and the offices of the Seattle-King County Health Department. The Carolyn Downs Family Medical Center offers health services to infants and children, adolescents, adults and seniors. It also offers health care for the homeless. Services are provided on a sliding fee scale based on household size and income.

The Carolyn Downs Family Medical Center is one of the Country Doctor Community Health Centers and is a federally qualified clinic.

Bus 27 to 22nd Avenue
(30, 47, 64 ,65, 66, 88, 99, 101)

CAROLYN DOWNS
May 18, 1953 – July 17, 1978

CAROLYN DOWNS was born May 18, 1953, in Marshall, Texas and came with her family to Seattle in 1964. She was the twelfth of the 16 children born to Johnny and Isadora Downs.

Ms. Downs attended Washington Junior High School and graduated in the class of 1971 from Garfield High School. She was a serious student and performed well academically. In 1972 she became passionately involved with the Black Panthers because of her strong interest in helping black people in the Central Area.

13

She was a lively volunteer, collecting donations and cooking for the free breakfast program, serving community dinners, working with the clothing bank, driving the Black Panther van to prisons for family visitations and assisting in the pest control program.

Ms. Downs had a warm and pleasing personality which made her popular in the organization and in the community she served. She had exceptional organizational skills and was always successful in securing volunteer cooks for the many community picnics and dinners she arranged.

She was also very active in the organization and the program of the Sidney Miller Free Medical Clinic, the forerunner of the Carolyn Downs Medical Center. She served as assistant to Elmer Dixon, the director of the clinic.

In addition to these activities, Miss Downs found time to attend Seattle Central Community College.

She became ill in 1978. In a few short weeks she succumbed to cancer. She is buried in Mount Pleasant Cemetery.

(21, 88, 89, 99)

◈ DOUGLASS – TRUTH LIBRARY ◈

A STATELY, OBLONG STRUCTURE with red tile roof has sat serenely on the corner of 23rd Avenue and East Yesler Way since 1914. This library building is unique among all the libraries in the city because it was built totally by city funds during the time of the Carnegie Foundation's construction of libraries.

Henry Yesler donated the property at 3rd Avenue, Jefferson Street and Yesler Way for a public library in 1889. The city traded the property to the Park Department and purchased a larger site at 23rd Avenue and Yesler Way in 1912. The Italian Renaissance style building was opened in 1915 and during its 70 years has faithfully served a changing ethnic community: Jewish, Japanese and black.

Until 1975, the library was named the Yesler Branch in honor of Seattle pioneer Henry Yesler. As the neighborhood became predominately black, Black Friends of Yesler Branch requested that the name be changed to reflect the changing population. Names were submitted and an equal number of votes were cast for Sojourner Truth and Frederick Douglass. On December 5, 1975, the name of the library was changed to Douglass-Truth by proclamation of Mayor Wes Uhlman.

Colorful portraits of the two abolitionists painted by artist Eddie Walker are on display in the building. A bronze plaque with a portrait of Henry Yesler hangs in the entrance.

In 1965, members of Alpha Kappa Alpha, a black women's sorority, donated more than 300 books to begin the "Negro Life and History Collection." With the help of Black Friends of Yesler Branch and later with a Library Services and Construction Act grant received in 1984, the African American Collection began to expand rapidly. It is now a major regional resource with holdings of over 6,000 volumes.

On September 17, 1988, the Douglass-Truth Library was rededicated after a major renovation made possible by Seattle 1-2-3 bond funds and generous contributions to the library renaissance fund.

Bus 27 to 23rd Avenue

(116, 124)

FREDERICK DOUGLASS
February 14, 1817 – February 20, 1895

FREDERICK AUGUSTUS WASHINGTON BAILEY was born a slave in Tuckahoe, Maryland. His mother, who died when he was seven years old, had called him her "little Valentine" and so he chose February 14th for his birthday.

In slavery he led a very hard life, sleeping on the floor, wearing few clothes in winter and fighting over food with the dog. The daughter of the plantation owner found him appealing and arranged for him to be the companion of her nephew in Baltimore. There he learned how to read and write and led a fairly pleasant life. Unfortunately, when he was 16, his benefactor died and he was ordered back to the plantation.

After a few aborted attempts, he escaped in 1838. In New Bedford, Massachusetts he changed his name to Douglass for fear of being discovered by slave hunters. He met the noted abolitionist William Lloyd Garrison and began speaking to audiences about his experiences as a slave. He spoke so eloquently that some people doubted his slavery past. This prompted him to write and publish *Narrative of the Life of Frederick Douglass, An American Slave* in 1845.

He traveled to England where friends there bought his freedom and he returned to the United States in 1847, settling in Rochester, New York. There he founded *The North Star*, an anti-slavery newspaper. His home became a station in the underground railroad system.

Mr. Douglass continued his eloquent oratory and writing, concerning himself with the abolition of slavery, equal rights for women and Native Americans and the ending of the death penalty. He encouraged President Lincoln to free the slaves and during the Civil

War he helped recruit black men for the Union Army. From 1881 to 1886 he served as recorder of deeds in the District of Columbia and was U.S. minister to Haiti from 1889 to 1891.

His home in Anacostia, Maryland is preserved as part of the National Park System.

(5, 10, 15, 18, 22)

SOJOURNER TRUTH
1797 – November 26, 1883

SOJOURNER TRUTH was born a slave in Ulster County, New York. Her first owners were Dutch and she spoke a Dutch jargon when, at age nine, she was sold to English owners. By 1827, when New York passed an emancipation act, she had been sold a number of times, had married and borne five children.

Formerly known as Isabella Baumfree or Isabella Van Wagen, she changed her name to Sojourner Truth in 1843. This new name would identify her purpose: to travel about and bring people the truth about the Holy Spirit. By this time she had moved to New York City, had worked in many menial jobs and had involved herself in religious movements. She became an itinerant Pentecostal preacher who drew large crowds in evangelistic movements because of her exceptional oratory skills.

As a very spiritual woman, she was attracted to a number of adventist groups and in many instances was one of the few black women active in them. Through these associations she began to meet feminists and abolitionists such as Frederick Douglass and

William Lloyd Garrison. She became excited about their mission and added her fervent and enthusiastic oratory to anti-slavery and feminist causes. She was the first black woman orator to receive wide attention.

Her fame spread and she met with President Lincoln in 1864. She remained in Washington, D. C. to help improve the living conditions of black people there and to help escaped slaves from the south to find jobs and housing. Conditions of black people were so miserable that Ms. Truth petitioned Congress for lands in the west to resettle her people. Nothing came of the idea, although she traveled the country seeking support.

. In her last years she continued speaking for the rights of women and black Americans. "Stretch out your hand in brotherhood to the colored people," she said. "We are all the children of one Father in heaven." She died in Battle Creek, Michigan and is buried there.

(4, 13, 22, 26)

✥ Edwin T. Pratt Park ✥

THIS 5.5 ACRE PARK is bounded by 20th Avenue South, East Yesler Way, South Washington Street and 18th Avenue South. It lies companionably near the Langston Hughes Cultural Arts Center, Bryant Manor, an apartment complex owned and sponsored by the First African Methodist Church and Kawabe House, a moderate income retirement home.

Entering the park on the path at its northeast corner one will find barbecue stoves and picnic tables scattered beneath maple and sycamore trees. The colorful Dr. Blanche Lavizzo Water Play Area is located to the south on the park grounds. Strolling farther along on the path, one will find an active play area for children, complete with tire swings, sandbox, merry-go-round, spider climb and monkey bars. In the south west corner of the park, dense with London Plane trees, are more benches and tables. A fenced garden of vegetables and flowers is located on the 18th Avenue South border. South of this area is a covered basketball court well used by neighborhood residents. The large grassy area to the east of the basketball court is often used for concerts, festivals and other community gatherings.

The park site was bought by the city in 1958 as part of the grounds for the Washington Junior High School, one block to the east. In 1966 it was chosen as the site for a park since the school had been rebuilt further south on Jackson.

Financed by funds from Forward Thrust and Urban Renewal, the park was developed between 1972 and 1979. It was designed by the firm of Woo and Park.

In 1976 the Park Board began considering the name of Edwin T. Pratt for the park. The naming was to be contingent upon concurrence by the Seattle Urban League and then only if the development was to be part of a healthy, economic neighborhood improvement program. When the executive committee of the League endorsed the choice and plans for the neighborhood were approved, the park was named in tribute to the slain civil rights leader.

Bus 27 to 20th Avenue South

(19, 112, 122)

⋘ THE PRATT FINE ARTS CENTER ⋙

THE PRATT FINE ARTS CENTER, a facility of the City of Seattle Department of Parks and Recreation, is located in the old Wonder Bread Bakery garage at 1902 South Main and is a place where people of all backgrounds can learn and work together in the visual arts. It was named in 1976. Remodeling began in 1977 and the facility opened in 1979.

Budget cuts in 1982 ended City funding of the Center. It is now incorporated as a non-profit organization called City Art Works at Pratt and is charged reduced rent by the City.

Through tuition, special events and contributions, the Center is able to operate its classes in glass blowing, glass arts, sculpture, metal arts, jewelry, painting, drawing and print making.

The instructors are professional working artists who teach from first-hand experience. The independent study and studio rental program is the only one of its kind in the Northwest.

The Center provides an opportunity for purchase of multi-media fine arts at its annual holiday sale in December and again at its auction which is held each May.

Bus 14 to 20th Avenue South. Walk north one block.
Bus 27 to 20th Avenue South. Walk south two blocks to South Main.
(109)

EDWIN T. PRATT
December 6, 1930 – January 26, 1969

SEATTLE WAS BLANKETED IN SNOW that January night in 1969 when Edwin T. Pratt was shot and killed in the doorway of his home by an unknown assailant. The city was shocked by the murder of this man whose voice was one of calm during the racial turmoil of the 1960s. Funeral services were held at St. Mark's Cathedral and his body was interred there.

Mr. Pratt was Executive Director of the Seattle Urban League. He lived in Seattle a little over 12 years, yet his leadership in human and civil rights have left an imprint on the fabric of life in the city. A committed integrationist, he believed that the problems of race could only be solved through integrated efforts.

Housing discrimination and de facto segregated schools were in place when Mr. Pratt arrived in Seattle in 1956. Through his leadership the League grew from a staff of five to one of 25 and changes began to take place.

To ease segregation in schools Mr. Pratt supported the Triad Plan, a proposal for reorganizing Seattle's elementary schools developed

23

by an Urban League committee and which became a turning point and hallmark in the continuing struggle against de facto segregation and for quality multi-racial education. He also conducted quiet negotiations with the University of Washington, urging the school to improve minority opportunity.

In housing he consistently pushed for integrated neighborhoods and promoted Operation Equality, the League's fair housing listing service and sponsor of a federal program encouraging home ownership by low income families.

Mr. Pratt was born in Miami, Florida, attended Clark College in Atlanta, Georgia, and received his master's degree in Social Work from Atlanta University. He joined the Urban League and served in Cleveland and Kansas City before being appointed Community Relations Secretary of the Seattle Urban League in 1956. Five years later he became Executive Director, exerting wise and compassionate leadership.

A catalyst and a negotiator, Edwin T. Pratt led Seattle on a higher road in race relations and as a local cleric commented, "His example should not be lost upon future generations who should recall his effort and glory that he once lived among us."

(34, 40, 41, 42, 50, 68, 76, 92, 105)

✥ Flo Ware Park ✥

*L*OCATED ON THE SOUTHEAST CORNER of 28th Avenue South and South Jackson Street, this tiny urban park will catch your eye in summer because of the cloud of burgundy leaves on the plum trees which shield it from neighboring traffic. Two huge catalpa trees border the park on the west and a lone pear tree is in its center.

An undulating concrete wall surrounds a sand bed. There are swings, slides, climbers, a merry go round and a basketball hoop for the neighborhood children. A bench, a picnic table, a stove and a water fountain complete the picture. On some summer days up to 25 youngsters from toddlers to teenagers enjoy this compact play area.

The 21,600 square foot park was purchased for $46,000 with Forward Thrust funds in 1969. William Talley was the landscape architect.

When Flo Ware died in 1981, there was an outpouring of feeling

from the community that she be memorialized. In 1982 the minia-
ture park was named for her.

Bus 14 to 28th Avenue South.

(19, 29, 122)

FLORASINA WARE
December 7, 1912 – March 17, 1981

FLO WARE was the quintessential activist.
She was known for raising a strong and
logical voice on behalf of children, the
elderly and the poor. She possessed an abid-
ing faith in people's ability to find a better way for the downtrodden.
Above all, she was clear sighted, direct and forthright in her beliefs.

Born in Fort Worth, Texas, she moved about with her family in a
specially equipped railroad car provided by the company for which
her father worked. Until high school she never went to the same
school for more than a few months. She attended college for a short
time, married and moved to Tacoma. She moved to Seattle in 1947.

In the early 1950s, dissatisfied with the quality of Central Area
schools, she decided to press school officials to work harder for
improvements. She was arrested once for passing out leaflets in front
of Horace Mann Elementary School. She continually agitated in a
calm, positive manner for social change.

Ms. Ware was known to be a very secure person with little interest in material possessions. Her high regard for people of all races,
religions and economic classes caused her to devote countless hours
to many worthy causes, particularly those relating to education,
health, the elderly and jobs for the poor.

26

Flo Ware represented Seattle in numerous national conferences on programs from Head Start to support for the aged. She served on innumerable national and local boards and received over 75 awards for her community work. She was an organizer of the Central Area School Board, the Foster Parent Association, spearheaded the Meals on Wheels Program for the elderly and had a radio talk show from 1968 to 1979 on KRAB.

In addition to community and national activities, Ms. Ware raised 20 foster children and was a mainstay on the Seattle King County Economic Opportunity Board during the War on Poverty years.

Flo Ware died on March 7, 1981. The mass of Christian burial was held at St. Therese Parish and her interment was at Mt. Pleasant Cemetery in Seattle.

(29, 59, 78, 123)

✥ Gideon-Mathews Gardens ✥

*T*his housing facility for low income seniors and disabled residents was dedicated on September 13, 1986. It is located at 24th Avenue South and South Jackson Street. A plaque in the lobby states that it was dedicated to the memory of Russell S. Gideon and Henrietta Mathews whose vision, courage and commitment were the gifts to a grateful Seattle. The developers of the facility were Jimmie Sumler and Dave Best of Promenade 23 Associates. The contractor was Luther Carr of Urban Construction and the architect was Thomas Harader of H.M. Company Inc.

The 45 unit building is under the management of the Seattle Housing Authority, a municipal corporation created in 1939 by the Seattle City Council under state law RCW 35.82 to provide low-rent housing and related services for low-income Seattle residents. Rental income and the U.S. Department of Housing and Urban Development (HUD) provide the majority of the Authority's revenue. Rents are 29% of the income of each resident in the senior housing.

Gideon-Matthews Gardens has 41 one bedroom units and four two bedroom units. Each unit has a living room, kitchen and bath. Amenities for residents include a large recreation room, a community room and kitchen, an exercise room, a laundry room and attractive seating areas on each floor.

The grounds are nicely landscaped with graceful birch trees, hearty rhododendrons and beds of cotoneaster. There is a parking lot on the north side of the building. On the southeast corner of the building is a lattice enclosed area with benches, tables and outdoor stoves for picnics or informal gatherings.
Bus 14 to 23rd Avenue. Walk east one block.
Bus 4 to South Jackson. Walk east one block.

(54, 85, 110)

RUSSELL GIDEON
October 9, 1904 – September 29, 1985

A COMMUNITY LEADER and a man of great energy and charm, Russell Gideon used these personal attributes to advantage in pursuing his many humanitarian and business interests.

Born in Liverpool, Nova Scotia, Canada, he moved with his family to Calgary, Alberta when he was nine years old. While growing up there he was an all star athlete in hockey, baseball, track and football. By the time he was 15 he was working as a drug store delivery boy after school and then playing drummer on weekends in a five piece band which he organized.

In 1932 Mr. Gideon left Calgary for Boston in order to become a pharmacist. When Massachusetts pharmacy schools finally admitted blacks, he entered and graduated from Western Massachusetts School of Pharmacy in 1941. During World War II he served as a technical sergeant in the 366th Infantry Medical Corps in Africa and Italy. He and his wife, Lillian, moved to Seattle in 1946. He bought a drug store at 22nd Avenue and East Madison Street and operated it until 1963.

A pioneer in senior housing, Mr. Gideon built the Elizabeth James House, named for his mother, at 23rd Avenue East and East Madison Street. He was past president of the East Madison-East Union Commercial Club and the originator of the Central Area's Seafair Mardi Gras festivities. He served on numerous boards among them being Florence Crittenden Home, Seattle Urban League, Foundation for International Understanding through Students at the University of Washington and the East Madison YMCA where he directed fund raising for the swimming expansion. In 1963 Governor Albert Rossellini appointed him to the Washington State Board of Prison Terms and Paroles. He was a charter member of the Central Area Kiwanis Club and a trustee at Mt. Zion Baptist Church.

National honor came to him as Sovereign Grand Commander of the United Supreme Council Ancient and Accepted Scottish Rite of Freemasonry, Prince Hall Affiliation, Northern Jurisdiction. In that post, he headed the 22,000 33rd-degree Prince Hall Masons north of the Mason-Dixon Line. A bust was commissioned in 1984 honoring his reign and was placed in the Masonic Cathedral's "Hall of Fame" in Philadelphia. In 1977 and until his death, he was recognized yearly by *Ebony* magazine as one of the nation's 100 most influential black citizens. Funeral Services were held at Mount Zion Baptist Church with interment at Sunset Hills Memorial Park in Bellevue.

(43, 91, 104)

30

Henrietta Mathews
July 15, 1915 – April 22, 1983

Henrietta mathews arrived in Seattle in 1957 with her husband, Meredith and two young sons. Friends remember her wide, pleasant smile, her dignified and gentle manner and her hazel eyes. With a career in social work and a passion for fair treatment for the young and the elderly, she made a distinct contribution to the betterment of life in Seattle.

Born in Columbus, Ohio, she received her B.A. degree in Business Administration at Ohio State University, a Masters in Social Work from the University of Oklahoma and a Masters in Education from San Jose State.

From 1949 to 1957 she was a Case Worker at the Oklahoma State Department of Public Welfare dealing mostly with child welfare. She began her distinguished career in Seattle in 1958 with the King County Juvenile Court as Probation Officer. From 1959 to 1965 she served as Case Worker with the Lutheran Family and Children Service and was Interim Supervisor of Adoptions and Field Work Instructor for students from the University of Washington School of Social Work. For the next three years she was branch executive of the East Side YWCA. Here she inaugurated a most successful program which provided education for unwed mothers. This program was adopted by the Seattle Public Schools as its first continuing education program for unwed mothers. In 1968 Mrs. Mathews joined the Seattle Public Schools as coordinator of school district programs and activities related to minority racial groups. During her eight year

31

tenure she supervised the tutoring of low achieving students, coordinated the voluntary racial transfer program and the District's Human Relations Training Unit.

After her retirement she worked incessantly as a volunteer to the aged, serving on the local and national Older Women's League and the Seattle King County Advisory Council on Aging. Governor John Spelman recognized her dedication and service by appointing her to the State Advisory Council on Aging.

Mrs. Mathews was a member of the Delta Sigma Theta Sorority and served on the boards of the NAACP and the Seattle Urban League. She died in Seattle and services were held at St. Marks Cathedral. She is buried at Sunset Hills Memorial Park in Bellvue.

(38, 79, 80)

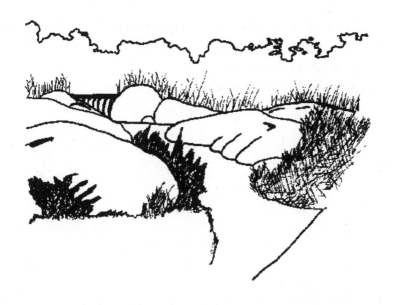

⪻ JIMI HENDRIX VIEWPOINT ⪼

AT THE WOODLAND PARK ZOO a series of large, smooth stones are clustered together. Here children gambol happily to view the zebras, giraffes and antelopes in the African Savannah. Other visitors may stand quietly and thoughtfully. One large brass star on a stone is engraved with the words, "This viewpoint was funded by worldwide donations to KZOK radio in the memory of Jimi Hendrix and his music."

The area is full of lush plants with purple leaves to suggest the song *Purple Haze*. Mr. Hendrix's fiery music is also recalled by a mosaic path of red flowers shaped like flames and a series of electrically heated rocks.

The controversial memorial was dedicated in 1982 after some fans voiced objections to the zoo location because they felt the jungle connotation was a slur to Hendrix' African ancestry.

Supporters of the site for the memorial say that the savannah is a celebration of African life and that the stones create a thoughtful environment for thousands of zoo visitors to enjoy.

Buses 5 and 43 to Woodland Park Zoo.

Follow signs to African Savannah.

(35, 60, 72)

JIMI HENDRIX
November 17, 1942 – September 18, 1970

J IMI HENDRIX was born in Seattle, grew up in the Central Area and became an internationally acclaimed guitarist and rock star. He was influenced as a child by his father's extensive record collection of rhythm and blues, by his mother's piano playing and by music at the Goodwill Baptist Church. As a youngster he went to Sick's Stadium one August afternoon in 1957, to hear Elvis Presley and watch his moves. He practiced these moves, using a broom for a guitar. When Jimi was 12, his father traded in his own saxophone for an electric guitar which he gave to his son to replace the broom.

Jimi Hendrix never learned to read music, but somehow, trained himself. He attended Garfield High School and played in rock groups around the city. He was a member of the Rocking Kings, which played for dances in places like Birdland, a club on East Madison Street. Leaving school at 17, he joined the Army where he learned to jump out of airplanes with the 101st Airborne Division. He received an early discharge after injuring his back in parachuting.

After his discharge, he toured the South in 1963 with a wide variety of acts. By 1964, he was in New York working with Ike and Tina

Turner, BB King, James Brown and Little Richard. In 1965, he formed his own group and was lured to London where he became an immediate sensation there and in Europe. His *Hey Joe* and *Purple Haze* became instant hits. By 1968, he was playing to standing room crowds in the United States. He last played in Seattle July 26, 1970, in Sick's Stadium.

Jimi Hendrix had an unusual approach to music and a fluent control over and use of distortion. His guitar of choice was a Fender Stratocaster. He soon became a guitarist's guitarist and influenced some of the most creative artists in pop music.

Mr. Hendrix got his star on the Hollywood Walk of Fame in 1991 and the following year was inducted into the Rock and Roll Hall of Fame. A bust by sculptor Jeff Day was placed in the Garfield High School Library in 1982.

On September 18, 1970, Jimi Hendrix was pronounced dead on arrival at St. Mary Abotts Hospital in London after overdosing on barbiturates. His funeral was held at the Dunlap Baptist Church in southeast Seattle and he is buried in Greenwood Cemetery in Renton.

(28, 45, 48, 57, 77)

⋐⋑ LANGSTON HUGHES ⋐⋑
CULTURAL ARTS CENTER

THE LANGSTON HUGHES CULTURAL ARTS CENTER is located at 104 17th Avenue South and is a designated Seattle landmark because of the unique architecture of the building. It was built for Congregation Bikur Cholim when the neighborhood was the center of Seattle's Jewish community. It was designed by the renowned theatre architect B. Marcus Priteca and built in 1914. According to the plaque hanging in the entrance to the theatre, the building represents an eclectic synthesis of neoclassical and Byzantine forms.

In 1971, the building was converted into a cultural arts center and named in 1973 for the nationally known black author whose picture hangs in the upstairs lobby. Under the auspices of the Seattle Park and Recreation Department, the center offers a variety of programs in theatrical, visual, literary and performing arts. It is one of the most popular and well-used buildings in the Park Department system.

Program offerings have included African culture classes for both adults and children, Tap Dance and Karate classes and a senior adult program. The Madrona Youth Theatre has been another program of the Center which boasts a 300 seat theatre.

Bus 27 to 17th Avenue South

(122)

LANGSTON HUGHES
February 1, 1902 – May 22, 1967

AN INTERNATIONALLY ACCLAIMED black poet, Langston Hughes wove the rhythms of the blues, jazz and bebop into his poetry about the life of black people and he did it with love, humor and optimism. He was the author of two autobiographies, several novels and for 23 years wrote the popular series of stories about Jesse Semple, the black Everyman.

Mr. Hughes was born in Joplin, Missouri and raised by his grandmother in Lawrence, Kansas because his parents had separated. A lonely child, living with an elderly woman in an all-white neighborhood, he felt an isolation which remained with him for years and caused him to turn to poetry to express his feelings.

He attended Columbia University and graduated from Lincoln University, Pennsylvania in 1929. Prior to his graduation, however, he had managed to have published many of his poems in magazines and to have two books published, *The Weary Blues* and *Fine Clothes to the Jew*. One of the major writers of the Harlem Renaissance, his

37

friends and associates included Countee Cullen, Zora Neal Hurston, Jesse Faucet and Arna Bontemps.

During the 1930s Mr. Hughes toured the South reading his poetry to create an interest in racial expression through books and to encourage young black literary talent. He also traveled extensively around the world, to Africa on a freighter, to Haiti, Cuba and to Paris where he worked in night clubs. He also ventured to Russia where he worked on a film project and to Italy where he wrote *I, Too, Am American*. But it was always to Harlem where he returned for the sounds and sights and problems of his people to transform into rhythmic, lyrical poetry.

In the last ten years of his life, Mr. Hughes devoted much of his energy to reviewing the fiction of young black writers including the novelist James Baldwin and the poet Gwendolyn Brooks. The author John Killens gave much credit to Mr. Hughes for the "gracious encouragement" to his writing.

Mr. Hughes died in Harlem at 65 years of age. His funeral was held there and, according to his instructions, a jazz band was hired to celebrate his memory.

(1, 11, 24)

MARTIN LUTHER KING ELEMENTARY SCHOOL

ON JANUARY 11, 1974, the pupils at the Harrison Early Childhood Center voted to change the name of their school to The Martin Luther King Early Childhood Center.

Located at 3201 East Republican Street, the school was first opened in September 1913, and named for Benjamin Harrison, 23rd president of the United States. Until 1958, it was a four-classroom structure and had varied grade configurations. It grew from serving grades one to four, to six grades. In 1932, the school was closed except for one first grade class and completely closed in the middle of the year. It reopened in the fall of 1936 serving grades one to three and later, after school enrollment increased, grades one to six.

Since 1958, students have enjoyed a modern addition that includes eight classrooms, a gymnasium, play court and lunchroom-auditorium. In 1968, Robert Bass became its first black principal to be followed by Louise McKinney, its second, in 1970, when the school became an early childhood center.

In September 1973, the students in Pennie Sheary's Room 10, having researched Harrison's life concluded that Dr. King's accomplishments might better suit the goals and aspirations of the school. They sent a letter to the School Board on September 21, 1973, requesting a name change. Ms. Sheary and her students presented their concern to the entire school. This resulted in a school wide election. The count was 203 for Martin Luther King and 164 for Benjamin Harrison. On March 27, 1974, the School Board authorized the name change, noting considerable neighborhood support and ample precedent for such an action.

Bus 11 to Lake Washington Blvd. East. Walk one block
to 32nd Avenue East, south two blocks to East Republican Street.

(14, 58, 73, 118)

❧ DR. MARTIN LUTHER KING, JR. ❧ MEMORIAL PARK

A TALL, BLACK GRANITE SCULPTURE and six semi-circular concrete tiers up a grassy hillside dominate this park on the corner of South Walker Street and Martin Luther King, Jr. Way.* Robert W. Kelly, the sculptor, was inspired by the "Mountaintop" speech Dr. King made in Memphis in 1968. The granite form symbolizes a mountain, difficult and perilous to climb, yet interspersed with plateaus of rest and reflection. The black granite is from Zimbabwe, where the Masona people have used it for centuries to carve intricate works of Shona sculpture which today are among the most valued in the world.

The park was dedicated on November 16, 1991, and is a place intended for quiet meditation on the teachings of Dr. King.

Visitors enter on a wide walkway and immediately find a sense of peace in the sound of water cascading from the memorial sculpture. Important stages of Dr. King's life are written on 12 bronze plaques set in the concrete surrounding the reflecting pool and quotations from some of his speeches are written on 12 bronze plaques set in a circular wall. Names of citizens and organizations supporting the park project are carved in bricks which form a part of the walkway around the fountain while major donors are listed on the donor wall.

At the entrance to the park another bronze plaque is set in a concrete wall. It lists the names of the 1994 recipients of the Content of Character Awards presented by the Seattle Community College District.

The Memorial Sculpture and its site are part of the Seattle Park and Recreation Department. The project development was funded by individual donors, corporate donors and major public support by King County, King County Arts Commission and City of Seattle Office of Neighborhoods.

Bus 4 to South Walker

*This eight mile street was once named Empire Way to honor James J. Hill whose efforts resulted in the construction of the transcontinental railroad to Seattle in 1891. In 1982, after a long struggle by Seattle businessman Eddie Rye, the street was renamed Martin Luther King, Jr. Way. In 1986, the King County Council passed Motion 6461 redesignating the namesake of King County to commemorate Dr. King rather than William Rufus DeVane King for whom the county was named in 1852. There is a bronze memorial plaque located on the first floor elevator lobby of the King County Courthouse at Third Avenue and James Street.

(107, 108, 115)

Dr. Martin Luther King, Jr.
January 15, 1929 – April 4, 1968

"Something must happen to awaken the dozing conscience of America before it is too late."

BORN IN ATLANTA, GEORGIA, the son of a Baptist minister, Martin Luther King, Jr. shook the conscience of this nation and prompted its leaders to make sweeping changes in civil rights laws. He spoke out eloquently about the plight of black people in the south and was inspired by Mohandas Gandhi to engage in nonviolent means for change.

In 1955, he led a bus boycott in Montgomery, Alabama to call attention to racial segregation in public transportation. Through sit-ins, boycotts, marches and imprisonment, he educated the nation and the world on the immorality of racial discrimination and stimulated all black Americans to seek their rightful place in this country.

Dr. King graduated from Morehouse College in Atlanta in 1948, received a BA degree in Divinity from Crozier Seminary in 1951 and a Doctorate in Systematic Theology from Boston University in 1954. He married Corretta Scott in 1953 and took over the pastorate of the Dexter Street Baptist Church in Montgomery, Alabama in 1954.

He was one of the founders of the Southern Christian Leadership Conference and its first president. He led the March on Washington in 1963 and the Selma to Montgomery March in 1965. The coveted Nobel Prize was presented to him in 1964.

Dr. King was assassinated in Memphis, Tennessee by James Earl Ray as he stood on the balcony of the Lorraine Motel reminding a musician to play *Precious Lord, Take My Hand* at the rally planned for garbage strikers that evening.

Among the Seattleites who knew Dr. King were Dr. Blanche Lavizzo, an elementary school mate in Atlanta, Dr. Samuel McKinney and Judge Jerome Farris, college classmates at Morehouse College. (2, 16)

❧ Medgar Evers Swimming Pool ❧

THE MEDGAR EVERS SWIMMING POOL is located north of Garfield High School on 23rd Avenue between East Jefferson and East Cherry Streets. It was the first of seven Forward Thrust pools to be built in the city between 1968 and 1980 and named upon community petition in 1969. The one million dollar project was financed by Forward Thrust and Model Cities and remains among the most impressive structures built in the civil rights leader's name in the United States. Others include an elementary school in Chicago and a recreation center in Jackson, Mississippi as well as streets in Compton, California and Greenville, Mississippi. In 1970 it became the first project with Model Cities support to receive an Honor Award from the U. S. Department of Housing and Urban Development in its Design Awards Program.

At the pool's dedication on April 26, 1970, Myrlie Evers, widow of Mr. Evers, said the swimming facility reminded her of her husband, "strong like a fortress". She said she hoped the pool would bring people together.

A mural bordering the entrance entitled "Omowale" by Curtis Barnes and Pauline Alley Barnes was dedicated in November 1974. It was a representation of black history and faded through the years. In 1996 the entrance to the pool was completely redesigned to provide a greenscape and handicapped access.

The 43 x 118 foot Medgar Evers Pool is operated by the Seattle Department of Parks and Recreation and offers adult, family and public swims, water exercise and masters workout. Swimming lessons are offered to children from birth to 17 years and to adults at all levels of mastery. The pool is available for rentals and is closed on Sunday.

Bus 48 to East Jefferson
Bus 3 to 23rd Avenue
Bus 4 to 23rd Avenue

(19, 56,122)

MEDGAR WILEY EVERS
July 2, 1925 – June 12, 1963

"When we get out of the army, we're going to straighten this out."

SERVING IN THE ARMY in 1943, Medgar Evers wrote this to his brother regarding the same inequality and same barriers there as in Mississippi. And when he returned he enrolled at Alcorn A & M College, convinced that a college education was essential to his growing determination to change social conditions for Mississippi blacks. He was single-minded in his efforts and demonstrated extraordinary courage.

Born in Decatur, Mississippi, Medgar Evers witnessed many atrocities to black people including the lynching of a family friend. He also saw nothing being done about it.

During his high school days he helped establish chapters of the National Association for the Advancement of Colored People in Mississippi. After graduating from college he worked for an insurance company in Mound Bayou, a tiny all-black village in the northwestern part of the state. He began economic boycotts against gas station owners who refused to let black people use their restrooms, revitalized NAACP chapters around the state and encouraged voter registration.

In 1954, after the University of Mississippi refused his admission to law school, he became the first paid field secretary in Mississippi for the NAACP. He and his wife Myrlie operated the office in Jackson. The specters of fear and violence were their constant companions because the white community felt a real threat to its status quo.

Determined, however to let the entire nation know about the atrocities committed against blacks, he investigated every crime and reported them to the NAACP national office. His investigation of the Emmet Till murder piqued the interest of northern newspapers and suddenly a national effort was under way to fight the injustices against black people in Mississippi.

Mr. Evers was a nonviolent person who believed two wrongs do not make a right. He was on the cutting edge of change and it cost him his life. In the early morning hours of a cloudless summer night he drove home after a late night mass meeting and was killed in his driveway by a single gunshot. Anger and shame spread throughout the country and turmoil erupted in the state as aroused black people demonstrated. On order of President John F. Kennedy, Mr. Evers' interment took place in Arlington National Cemetery.

(3, 7, 17)

⟨⟩ THE MEREDITH MATHEWS ⟨⟩
EAST MADISON YMCA

*T*HIS STURDY, MODERN STRUCTURE housing a gymnasium, swimming pool, activity rooms and offices was built in 1965 and designed by Leon Bridges. It was remodeled and enlarged in 1991. Located at 23rd Avenue and East Olive the site was formerly used as a tennis club by members of the community. The property was owned by the Colman family, long-time supporters of the YMCA. Members of the black community persuaded the owners to deed the property to the YMCA and in 1936 the modest building and grounds became a new branch of the Seattle YMCAs.

During the World War II years the East Madison YMCA became an Armed Services YMCA for black servicemen and catered largely to them. Under the leadership of John Copeland in the mid 1940s, the Y reached out to the schools and with increased youth programs began to attract more and more young people. The programs and the facility grew even more under the leadership of Meredith Mathews. Many of today's leading black professionals, community leaders and businessmen in Seattle were nurtured at this branch.

The present facility, with 12 staff members, offers classes in swimming, tai chi, aerobics, line dancing, senior exercises and computers. The Black Achievers Program provides an opportunity for young people to explore career opportunities. Volley ball, basketball and Double Dutch programs are available.

In December 1993, the YMCA of Greater Seattle Board of Directors named the branch The Meredith Mathews East Madison Branch YMCA in recognition of Mr. Mathews' outstanding contribution to the YMCA and to the Seattle community. This is the first YMCA facility of Greater Seattle to be named for an individual.
Bus 11 to 23rd Avenue East. Walk south one block to East Olive.
Bus 47 to East Olive
Bus 48 to East Olive

(102, 103)

MEREDITH MATHEWS
September 4, 1919 – March 10, 1992

MEREDITH MATHEWS was a friend to youth and his name was synonymous with the YMCA. A man of pleasant demeanor and personality, he began an association with the organization in 1937 as Director of the Spring Street YMCA in Columbus, Ohio and continued his professional career with the organization in Oklahoma City and McAlester, Oklahoma.

Mr. Mathews came to Seattle in October 1957, as Executive Director of the East Madison YMCA. The fund raising and business management skills he had developed in Oklahoma were used to expand services, memberships and programs at the Seattle branch. A new facility was built in 1965 after a successful Capital Funds Campaign under his leadership and with outstanding support from the community.

In recognition of his contributions to the organization and his loyalty to the YMCA family, Mr. Mathews was appointed Associate Executive of the Pacific Northwest Area Council of YMCAs in 1965. In 1971, he was named Regional Executive of the Pacific Region of YMCAs and was responsible for oversight of 126 facilities and programs in 11 states. He retired after 39 years of outstanding service to the YMCA.

Born in Thomaston, Georgia, Mr. Mathews received his high school education in Columbus, Ohio. He received his B.S. degree from Wilberforce University in Ohio and pursued graduate studies at Ohio University.

Mr. Mathews was uncommonly loyal, not only to family, but to friends and to just causes. He was a personal friend of Edwin T. Pratt and Randolph Carter and served on the boards of the Seattle Urban League and the Randolph Carter Center. He was a Mason, a member of Sigma Pi Phi Fraternity and prior to his death was the oldest living member of the Alpha Phi Alpha Fraternity in the Seattle area. Community groups as well as the YMCA awarded him for his service and for his leadership. Hundreds of people considered him a role model and an inspiration to them when they were children. In 1995, his name was placed in the YMCA Hall of Fame in Springfield, Massachusetts.

Mr. Mathews' death on March 10, 1992, was the result of injuries sustained during a robbery and assault in Seattle in June 1991. Funeral services were held at the First African Methodist Episcopal Church and interment was at Sunset Hills Memorial Park in Bellevue. (32, 102)

❧ ODESSA BROWN CHILDREN'S CLINIC ❧

*T*HE ODESSA BROWN CHILDREN'S CLINIC, which treats children throughout Seattle and King County, was developed cooperatively by the Seattle Model Cities Program, Children's Orthopedic Hospital and Medical Center and concerned citizens of the Central Area. It opened in 1970 at 2017 East Spruce Street and moved into its new building at 2101 East Yesler Way in 1980.

The clinic provides medical, dental and other support services. Dr. Blanche Lavizzo, a black woman pioneer in pediatrics, was its first medical director and the inspiration for its motto: *Quality care with dignity.*

In 1994 the clinic, a satellite of Children's Hospital, became a partner in the Central Area Health Care Center with Carolyn Downs Family Medical Center and the Seattle-King County Department of Health. The building was enlarged and remodeled to accommodate the two new health entities.

Photographs of Odessa Brown and Dr. Blanche Lavizzo hang in
the clinic. A James Washington sculpture entitled "My Testimony
in Stone" is located on the right of the main entrance.
Bus 27 to 22nd Avenue.

(27, 97)

ODESSA M. BROWN
April 30, 1920 – October 15, 1969

A S A COMMUNITY ORGANIZER for the
Central Area Motivation Program
during the 1960s, Odessa Brown was a
staunch supporter of a health care facility
for children in the Central Area.

She worked in the neighborhoods to make residents aware of the
needs of the area and to express these needs to the planners of Model
Cities. Ms. Brown was a quiet, private woman but when she spoke
people listened. It was always about health care for children. So it
was that when the Model Cities presented its health plan, it was for
a children's clinic.

Born April 30, 1920, in Des Arc, Arkansas, she came to Seattle in
1963 as a licensed beautician having trained in the C. J. Walker
Beauty School in Chicago. As a mother of four, she worked hard to
support her family through work in the Central Area Motivation
Program and as a beautician at Les Coffie's DeCharlene Fashion
Beauty Salon at 2105 East Union.

Friends and associates were unaware of the debilitating illness she
suffered. When she missed a meeting or did not report to work on
rare occasions no one assumed anything more than a minor prob-

lem. It came as a surprise to all who knew her that she had leukemia and had had it for much of the time she had been associated with CAMP.

Odessa Brown died on October 15, 1969. She is buried at Holyrood Cemetery in Seattle. When the time came to name the children's clinic which opened its doors in 1970, there was never a question from the organizers but that it be the Odessa Brown Children's Clinic.

(27,63,87,95)

❧ Peppi's Playground ❧

A DELIGHTFUL PATCH OF GREEN, east of Leschi Elementary School between East Spruce Street and Lake Dell, awaits children and parents seeking adventure or quiet contemplation. The 2.7 acre plot, designed by Donald Sakuma, is filled with cedars, pines, a magnificent magnolia and bordered on the east with madrona trees.

There are restrooms and a paved path for bicycling or short walks. At the southeast corner of the park is a wading pool edged with cement and a low brick wall, perfect for resting or watching children at play.

Through a colorful wall with a circular opening youngsters enter a large sandlot with climbers, hobby horses on springs, a sliding board, a swing and a seesaw. Steps lead up to a trail winding a short distance through a fenced wooded glade not unlike a fairyland.

This playground siting is the result of community efforts begun in

1953 with a petition for a children's facility in Frink Park. Although the neighborhood was deficient in playgrounds, the Planning Commission recommended against the site because it did not provide adequate space.

In 1968, civic and business leaders in Seattle's Forward Thrust Program, working with neighborhood representatives, came up with a list of sites deemed desirable for development as parks. This lovely site, selected by the Leschi Community and Park Board, was acquired in 1970 and named in 1971 by the students at Leschi Elementary School.

Bus 27 to Lake Dell Avenue.

(19, 122)

Peppi Braxton
December 13, 1963 – July 3, 1971

PEPPI BRAXTON was a first grader at Leschi Elementary School who was killed on his bicycle after he sped down a driveway in the back of his home into the path of an automobile on Yakima Place South.

Although Peppi lived in the Colman Elementary School area, he attended kindergarten and first grade at Leschi Elementary School at the request of his parents.

He was an attentive, alert student, admired by his teachers and a favorite of the other students. A teacher called one day to tell his mother, "The children look to Peppi to lead them and to take care of them." The students at Leschi voted to have their playground named for him.

(82)

⋘ Powell Barnett Park ⋙

THIS 4.4 ACRE PARK is located on Martin Luther King Jr. Way between East Jefferson and East Alder Streets. The property originally was chosen by the City Planning Commission as the East Junior High School Site. It was developed as a running track and athletic field for Garfield High School.

By 1962 Garfield had obtained a track closer to the school and the property was sold to the Park Department in 1966. Playground improvements were made through the Central Area Motivation Project in 1967 based upon a design by landscape architect William Talley.

In 1969 the children at Leschi Elementary School named the park for the organizer and first president of the Leschi Improvement Council.

Park visitors and motorists driving along the busy arterial adjacent to it, likely will notice first the unusual castle structure that houses the restrooms near the colorful climbers and sandlot on the southwest corner. Nearby are a wading pool and basketball court. Picnic tables and benches are well placed on the contoured grassy grounds shaded by pine, oak and maple trees. A long, circling path awaits walkers in search of quiet relaxation. The hilltop on the southeast corner offers benches and a lovely view.

Bus 3 to Martin Luther King Jr. Way. Walk south one block.
Bus 84 to Martin Luther King, Jr. Way. Walk south one block.

(19, 25, 122)

POWELL BARNETT
August 2, 1883 – March 16, 1971

BORN IN BRAZIL, INDIANA, Powell Barnett moved to Roslyn, Washington in 1889. His father, an ex-slave, had been among many black miners recruited to work in the coal mines of Washington State. Powell, as a teenager, also worked in the Roslyn coal mines and played in the "colored" band.

Powell Barnett came to Seattle in 1906 because he thought the city offered greater opportunities. He began working for Barary Asphalt Paving Company as sub-foreman putting in new street car lines. Later he worked for the General Engineering Construction Company which built the Waldorf Hotel at 7th and Pike and the Perry Hotel on 9th and Madison. He served as a clerk for State Senator Frank Connor and retired at 71 as a maintenance man at the King County Courthouse.

A man of many interests and great energy, much of which were directed toward improving race relations and civic unity, Mr. Barnett became a leader in the community. He organized the Leschi Improvement Council and became its first president in 1967; led in organizing the East Madison YMCA and served as chairman of the board; and chaired a committee that revised the Seattle Urban League thus saving its membership in the Community Chest.

A sousaphone player and a firm believer in racial integration, he was instrumental in uniting blacks and whites in the YMCA, the USO and the local musicians unions. He was the first black person to become a member of the once all-white Musicians Union, Local 76. A star baseball player, he organized a semi-pro baseball Umpires Association in Seattle, served as executive secretary from 1944 until 1961 and secured affiliation with the National Association of Umpires.

Mr. Barnett received numerous awards for outstanding civic contributions from many associations in the city, including the King County Council on Aging, Jackson Street Community Council, Seattle Urban League, the Mayor and City Council.

Mr. Barnett died in 1971 having lived most of his life in the Leschi Community. He is buried at Mt. Pleasant Cemetery.

(25, 53, 55, 74, 96)

⇜ PRENTIS FRAZIER PARK ⇝

*T*HE PRENTIS FRAZIER PARK is located at 24th Avenue East and East Harrison Street. Tucked at the bottom of a sloping hill, this tiny park is popular with children.

Slides and climbers for toddlers are conveniently arranged in a circular sand area around which curves an asphalt walk and play area. Older children have access to a basketball hoop. Benches, a water fountain and outdoor lighting are other features of this play area. Oak and maple trees provide a buffer from the sound of traffic on 23rd Avenue above. The 0.3 acre park, formerly known as Harrison Street Mini Park, was bought with Forward Thrust funds in 1970 and designed by David Jensen. After recommendations by neighbors, friends and relatives, the park was renamed in 1983 for the business man who had lived nearby.

Bus 48 to East Harrison. Walk east one block.

(19, 122)

PRENTIS I. FRAZIER
November 17, 1880 – October 11, 1959

PRENTIS I. FRAZIER came to Seattle in 1916 with little formal education but with an innate business sense and a desire to promote financial prosperity for the small black community he found here and for himself and his family.

He was born in the community of Magnolia Springs, Jasper County, Texas to Martha and Armstead Frazier, both former slaves. At an early age he left his farm home to seek his fortune, first in Beaumont and later in Dallas, Texas. After his business ventures in banking and the operation of a boarding house failed, he and his wife Clara headed north to eventually settle in Seattle where he attained financial success.

For almost 40 years, Mr. Frazier operated in real estate, insurance, bail bonds and investments. His first office was in the Pacific Building at Second Avenue and Yesler. Always alert to opportunities to promote other business in the small black community, he helped organize Blackwell and Johnson Undertakers on East Marion between 12th and 13th Avenues in 1920. At 21st Avenue and East Madison, he and Attorney Clarence Anderson opened the Anzier Movie Theatre in 1925.

Later in the 1920s he and William Wilson started and published a small black oriented newspaper, *The Seattle Enterprise*, which was later renamed the *Northwest Enterprise* and ran until the early 1950s. In the early 1940s he went into the bail bond business with offices in the Lyon Building at Third and James.

Prentis I. Frazier was an active member of the Republican Party and was a member and generous contributor to the First African Methodist Episcopal Church.

Mr. Frazier always lived in the Central Area, residing the last ten years of his life at 410 23rd Avenue East. When the gully behind his home was designated a mini-park, relatives and neighbors recommended it be named for him because of his contribution to the community as a philanthropist and business entrepreneur. He is interred at Sunset Hills Memorial Park in Bellevue.

(81, 113, 114)

⋘ RANDOLPH CARTER CENTER ⋙

HE RANDOLPH CARTER CENTER property at the southeast corner of 23rd Avenue South and Yesler Way was purchased through the city of Seattle for a nominal price and a building to house a sheltered workshop was financed through grants from the federal government and individual contributions. The facility opened in 1976 and provided on the job training for mentally, emotionally or physically handicapped people as well as job placement and vocational training. Unfortunately, due to diminished federal and state financial support, the center was forced to close its doors in the summer of 1986.

In August 1988, the building reopened as the Catholic Community Services at the Randolph Carter Center. The Catholic Community Services was established in 1937 to serve the needs of children and families. Over the years, through support from United Way, city and state, it has become the largest private multi-service agency in Washington State, touching the lives of over 50,000 individuals.

A portrait of Randolph Carter and a plaque about his life hang in the lobby of the building.

Bus 27 to 23rd Avenue

(86, 98)

RANDOLPH WARREN CARTER
November 15, 1913 – February 9, 1970

R ANDOLPH WARREN CARTER was born in Riverside, California, the first of nine children. He received his B.A. degree in sociology from Whittier College after setting track records for himself and his alma mater. In 1938 the year he graduated, he won the Small College Relay Championship for the United States, a record that stood for 20 years. In 1981 he was inducted into the Whittier Hall of Fame.

From 1943 to 1944, Mr. Carter served as Director of the Market Street United Service Organization in Stockton, California and then in Los Angeles as a group worker for the All Nations Foundation. For six years he coordinated the work of 15 agencies offering integrated program services in the city of Los Angeles.

After completing his Masters Degree in Social Work from the University of Southern California in 1952, Mr. Carter came to Seattle and launched a successful career in the state. He served as Community Relations Secretary at the Seattle Urban League for three years then moved on to become Juvenile Probation Officer for the King County Juvenile Court from 1955 to 1959. In 1965 Mr.

Carter was appointed Executive Secretary of the Washington State Board Against Discrimination.

The last years of his life were devoted to the employment and training services for the disadvantaged and the disabled through the State Division of Vocational Rehabilitation. It was through this association that his final career fulfillment was realized.

In 1967 with Edward Grinrod, he developed a center for the handicapped at the corner of 21st Avenue and East Spruce Street in an old warehouse building. Here with the use of simple machinery an enrollment of from 10 to 15 trainees was maintained. Some of the trainees were referred from Pacific Prevocational School, a Seattle School District program. From this simple beginning the workshop known as the Central Area Industrial Workshop was started. It was licensed under the State of Washington and received grants from the federal government. Three years after Mr. Carter's death in 1970 the facility was named Randolph Carter Industrial Workshop.

In 1976 the property at the corner of 23rd Avenue and East Yesler Way was purchased through the City of Seattle for a minimal price and a new home for the facility was constructed using grants from the federal government and individual contributions.

Mr. Carter is buried at Washington Park Cemetery.

(49 ,69, 70 ,86, 105)

⇜ Thurgood Marshall ⇝ Elementary School

*T*HIS 29,000 SQUARE FOOT brick school was built in 1991 as the new Colman Elementary School at a cost of $5.6 million. Mahlum and Nordfors were the architects and Ellis-Don Construction was the contractor. It is located at 2401 South Irving and its playground is on the I-90 freeway lid.

The school has 16 regular classrooms, two kindergartens, two resource rooms, one art/science room and five handicapped student classrooms. There are conferencing spaces, a library, administrative space, a kitchen and a staff lounge. The gymnasium/lunchroom/auditorium are available for community use.

In a new separate building, the East Madison YMCA operates a child care center which provides before/after school and all day care. There is a self-contained play yard for the children.

The first Colman Elementary School at 1515 24th Avenue South opened in 1909 and was named for Laurence J. Colman, a native of Scotland, who came to Seattle in 1869. He was an engineer who directed the building of many early sawmills in the Seattle area. The school was closed in the late 1970s and reopened as an alternative school. Colman was again closed in 1985 due to the construction of the last link of the I-90 freeway. This vacated building was occupied by a group of black activists seeking to establish an African American Cultural Museum.

In February 1996, Ed Jefferson, Principal of the new Colman Elementary School, submitted a proposal to the Seattle School Board to change the name of the school to Thurgood Marshall Elementary School. A public hearing was scheduled to seek community input on the proposal and in March 1996, the School Board voted unanimously for the name change to be effective September 1996.

Bus 4 to South Judkins. Walk south one block.
Bus 48 to South Judkins. Walk east on South Judkins one block;
south one block on 24th Avenue South to South Irving;
east on South Irving one block to the school.

(119, 120, 121)

THURGOOD MARSHALL
July 2, 1908 – January 24, 1993

President Lyndon Johnson nominated Thurgood Marshall to the United States Supreme Court in 1967. He became the first black man to serve on the highest court of the land. He served until 1991 when he resigned because of ill health.

Born in Baltimore, Mr. Marshall attended segregated schools there. He graduated from Lincoln University, Pennsylvania in 1930. After being denied entrance to the all-white University of Maryland Law School, he graduated from Howard University Law School, Washington, D. C. in 1933, ranking first in his class.

The next three years of private practice were financially difficult for he fought and won many legal battles without pay. In 1936 he began a long career with the National Association for the Advancement of Colored People, becoming its chief legal counsel in 1940.

Of the 32 cases he argued in the U.S. Supreme Court as the association's legal counsel, he won 29. Among them were cases the court declared unconstitutional: a Southern state's exclusion of black voters from primary elections (1944); racial restrictive covenants in housing (1948); and separate but equal facilities for black professional and graduate students in state universities (1950). In 1954 he argued and won the Brown v. Board of Education of Topeka which declared segregated education unconstitutional.

In 1961 President John F. Kennedy appointed Thurgood Marshall to the United States Court of Appeals, for the Second Circuit. He served there until 1965 when he was appointed United States Solicitor General.

Thurgood Marshall was a champion of civil rights and will long be remembered for his attacks on discrimination. When he died, his body lay in state in the Great Hall of the Supreme Court and over 20,000 mourners came to pay their last respects.

(6, 9 ,12, 23)

⋘ WILLIAM GROSE PARK ⋙

A<small>N ASPHALT PATH</small> curves through this fenced green park which sprawls between 30th Avenue East and 31st Avenue East on the block between East Howell Street and East Denny Way. A dramatic deodora cedar tree shades its eastern entrance while three graceful western red cedar trees border the west. The grassy slopes are perfect for small family picnics or games. Two benches face a bed of low shrubs. This is a sedate and secluded neighborhood park.

The 18,700 square foot site was purchased by the city in 1970 with funds from Forward Thrust and the Washington State Interstate Agency for Outdoor Recreation. The Madison Valley Concerned Citizens Organization was responsible for securing a $31,000 Community Development Block Grant for improvements to the park designed by Rosemary Wills, Parks Department Senior Landscape Architect.

The Black Heritage Society of Washington State and the Madison Valley Concerned Citizens supported the naming because it honors and acknowledges the important role that black people played in settling and developing Madison Valley. The park was dedicated in September 1983, and the Black Heritage Society and other interested citizens celebrated the occasion with a picnic on the grounds. A bronze plaque with an image of Mr. Grose and descriptive text was placed in the park by the Society.

Bus 2 to East Howell. Walk west to 31st Avenue East, then north a few feet.

(19, 33, 67, 122)

WILLIAM GROSE
1835 – July 27, 1898

IN 1851 Seattle's founders landed at Alki and less than a decade later William Grose arrived, becoming a successful businessman and one of the city's largest landowners and biggest taxpayers.

Mr. Grose (often spelled Gross) was 15 when he left his home in Washington, D.C. to join the U. S. Navy. During his naval career he made expeditions to the Arctic and also to Japan. But this was only the beginning of his adventures. He left the Navy for the gold mines of California, working around the Montezuma, Columbia and Sonora Districts and a number of other camps in that area.

Mr. Grose helped form an underground railroad to relieve those in slavery, even going to Panama to persuade officials not to send escaped slaves back to the South. Back in California he assisted in making arrangements for the settlement of black people in Victoria, B. C. and on the Fraser River.

Later, serving as steward on the seagoing vessel, The Constitution, which carried mail between Victoria, B. C. and Olympia, he had a fortuitous meeting with Governor Isaac Stevens. Mr. Grose found and kept safely a watch belonging to the governor who was so impressed with the man he urged him to move to Washington Territory.

This black Seattle pioneer was a big man in spirit and in body, weighing over 400 pounds and standing six feet four inches tall. He opened "Our House", a hotel and restaurant on Yesler Way, which became a popular stop for Seattle's mostly white populace. He also became a good friend of the city's prominent pioneer families. Stories abound about his generosity, integrity and honesty. One story, told by Attorney J. E. Hawkins, recounts how Mr. Grose sold his hotel for $5,000. It later burned in the 1889 fire. Mr. Grose found the new owner and returned the $5,000.

William Grose was the first black person to buy property in East Madison. He purchased a 12 acre tract from Henry Yesler for $1,000 in gold in 1882. His home, with slight alterations, still stands at 1733 24th Avenue. Mr. Grose was a Mason, a trustee of First African Methodist Episcopal Church and a member of the Washington Pioneer Association. Mr. Grose is buried in Lake View Cemetery on Capital Hill.

(20, 21, 33, 62, 71, 100)

❧ ADDRESSES ❧

AL LARKINS PARK: *34th Avenue and East Pike*

ALVIRITA LITTLE CENTER FOR GIRLS: *708 Martin Luther King, Jr. Way*

DR. BLANCHE LAVIZZO PARK: *22nd Avenue from East Yesler Way
to South Jackson Street*

DR. BLANCHE LAVIZZO WATER PLAY AREA: *20th Avenue South
and South Washington Street*

CAROLYN DOWNS FAMILY MEDICAL CENTER: *2101 East Yesler Way*

DOUGLASS-TRUTH LIBRARY: *2300 East Yesler Way*

EDWIN T. PRATT PARK: *18th Avenue South and South Washington Street*

FLO WARE PARK: *28th Avenue South and South Jackson Street*

GIDEON-MATHEWS GARDENS: *323 24th Avenue South*

JIMI HENDRIX VIEWPOINT: *NE 50th Street Entrance to the
Woodland Park Zoo in the African Savannah*

LANGSTON HUGHES CULTURAL ARTS CENTER: *17th Avenue South
and East Yesler Way*

MARTIN LUTHER KING ELEMENTARY SCHOOL: *3201 East Republican*

DR. MARTIN LUTHER KING, JR. MEMORIAL PARK: *Martin Luther King, Jr.
Way South and Walker Street*

MEDGAR EVERS POOL: *500 23rd Avenue*

MEREDITH MATHEWS East Madison YMCA: *1700 23rd Avenue*

ODESSA BROWN CHILDREN'S CLINIC: *2101 East Yesler Way*

PEPPI'S PLAYGROUND: *32nd Avenue and Spruce Street*

POWELL BARNETT PARK: *East Jefferson Street and
Martin Luther King, Jr. Way*

PRATT FINE ARTS CENTER: *1902 South Main*

PRENTIS FRAZIER PARK: *24th Avenue East and East Harrison Street*

RANDOLPH CARTER CENTER: *100 23rd Avenue South*

THURGOOD MARSHALL ELEMENTARY SCHOOL: *2401 South Irving Street*

WILLIAM GROSE PARK: *30th Avenue East between East Howell Street
and East Denny Way*

❧ REFERENCES ❧

Books

1. Berry, Faith. Langston Hughes: *Before and Beyond Harlem*. New York: Lawrence Hill, 1983.

2. Boates, Stephen. *Let the Trumpet Sound; the Life of Martin Luther King, Jr.* New York: Penguin, 1985.

3. Brown, Jennie. *Medgar Evers*. Los Angeles: Melrose Square, 1994.

4. Carleton, Mabel. *Sojourner Truth; Slave, Prophet, Legend*. New York: University Press. 1993.

5. Douglass, Frederick. *Autobiographies*. New York: Library of America, 1994.

6 Davis, Michael D. *Thurgood Marshall, Warrior at the Bar, Reel on the Bench*. Secaucus, N.J.: Carol Publishing Group, 1994

7. Evers, Mrs. Medgar. *For Us The Living*. Garden City, N.Y.: Doubleday, 1967.

8. Forward Thrust Committee. *Final Forward Thrust Progress Report: Through the Vision of the People*. Seattle. 1980.

9. Haskins, James. *Thurgood Marshall: A Life for Justice*. New York: Henry Holt, 1992.

10. Higgins, Nathan. *Slave and Citizen; The Life of Frederick Douglass*.

11. Hughes, Langston. *The Big Sea*. New York: Alfred Knopf, 1940.

12. Kallen, Stuart A. *Thurgood Marshall: A Dream of Justice for All*. Edina, MI: Abdo, 1993.

13. Krass, Peter.*Sojourner Truth; Anti-Slavery Activist*. New York: Chelsea House, 1988.

14. Levant, Sara, ed. *Seattle School Histories. 1869-1974*. Seattle: Seattle Public Schools, 1974.

15. Martin, Waldo E. *The Mind of Frederick Douglass*. Chapel Hill, N.C.: University of North Carolina Press, 1984.

16. McKissack, Patricia. *Martin Luther King, A Man to Remember*. Chicago: Childrens Press, 1984.

17. Metcalf, George. *Black Profiles*. New York: McGraw Hill, 1968.

18. Miller, Douglas T. *Frederick Douglass and the Fight for Freedom*. New York: Facts on File, 1988.

19. Morgan, Brandt. *Enjoying Seattle's Parks*. Seattle: Greenwood Publications, 1979.

20. Mumford, Esther. *Calabash; A Guide to the History, Culture and Art of African Americans in Seattle and King County Washington*. Seattle: Ananse Press, 1992.

21. Mumford, Esther. *Black Victorians*. Seattle: Ananse Press, 1980.

22. Painter, Nell. *Sojourner Truth: A Life, A Symbol*. New York: W. W. Norton, 1996.

23. Rowan, Carl. *Dream Makers: The World of Justice Thurgood Marshall*. Boston: Little Brown, 1993.

24. Rummel, Jack. *Langston Hughes*. New York: Chelsea House, 1988.

25. Vaughn, Wade. *Seattle Leschi Diary*. Seattle: Leschi Improvement Council. 1982.

25. Vaughn, Wade. *Seattle Leschi Diary*. Seattle: Leschi Improvement Council. 1982.
26. Washington, Margaret, ed. *Narrative of Sojourner Truth*. New York: Vintage Books, 1993.
27. Williams, De Charlene. *History of Seattle's Central Area*. Seattle: Central Area Chamber of Commerce. 1990.
28. Willix, Mary. *Jimi Hendrix: Voices from Home*. San Diego, CA: Creative Forces, 1995.

Newspaper Articles

29. Andrews, Paul. *"Lest it Escape Notice: May 8th was Flo Ware Day in Seattle."* Seattle Times 11 May 1982, p. C2.
30. Angelos, Constantine. *"One-Stop Medical Care a Step Closer."* Seattle Times. 27 March 1992, p. C3.32.
31. Angelos, Constantine. *"Water Park to Become Reality."* Seattle Times. 15 Dec. 1993, p. B1.
32. Birkland, Dave. *"Meredith Mathews, Longtime YMCA Executive Devoted to Helping Others."* Seattle Times. 14 March 1992.
33. Carson, Jerry. *"Mini-park Dedicated to Black City Pioneer, Big Landowner."* Seattle Times. 25 Sept. 1983, p. A16.
34. Evans, Walter. *"Bicentennial Biographies: Edwin T. Pratt."* Seattle Post Intelligencer. 19 Sept. 1975, p. 1.
35. Gray, Jeffrey. *"Hendrix Memorial: Garfield High's Most Famous Drop Out Gets a Spot at Zoo."* The Weekly. (Seattle, WA) 31 Mar 1982, p. 8-9.
36. Iwasaki, John. *"Area Honors Doctor Who Put Children First."* Seattle Post Intelligencer. 18 Dec. 1993, p. B1.
37. Johnson, Kathy Bunnell. *"Blanche Lavizzo, Clinic Director, Dies."* Seattle Times. 29 Aug. 1984, p. C4.
38. Jones, Marjorie. *"Agencies Provide Education for Unwed Mothers."* Seattle Times. Jan. 1968, p.35.
39. Mar, Andy. *"New Waterworks Aim to Please."* Seattle Times. 11 July 1995, p. B1.
40. Parks, Michael J. *"A Decade of Involvement in Rights' Movements."* Seattle Times. 2 Feb. 1969.
41. Raley, Dan. *"New Clues in 1969 Murder."* Seattle Post Intelligencer. 13 Dec. 1994, p. 1.
42. Smith, Lane. *"Pratt Left Guidelines to Erase Prejudice."* Seattle Times. 2 Feb. 1969, p. 1.
43. Stokes, Carl. *"Tribute to Russell Sidney Gideon."* U. S. Congressional Record (House). 2 Oct. 1985, p H8074.
44. Watson, Emmett. *"Ever Come Monday."* Seattle Post Intelligencer. 22 Jan. 1979, p. B1
45. *"Are You Experienced? (Born and Raised in the CA)"* Seattle Post Intelligencer. 6 Sept. 1968, Area 206, p. 2.
46. *"Best Squirt Gun in Town."* Seattle Post Intelligencer. 12 July 1995, p. B2.

47. *"Black Panthers to Investigate Shooting Death of Member."* Seattle Times. 3 Dec. 1968, p. 1

48. *"Blues Show Goes on with Hendrix."* Seattle Times. 7 Sept. 1968, p. 12.

49. *"Carter Says He Had Agreement to Quit."* Seattle Times. 29 May 1965, p. 56.

50. *"Clergymen of Three Faiths to Join in Pratt Rites".* Seattle Times. 28 Jan. 1969, p. 6.

51. *"Dr. Blanche Lavizzo of Children's Orthopedic."* Seattle Post Intelligencer. 29 Aug. 1984, p. D1

52. *"Dr. Blanche Lavizzo to Head MC's Odessa Brown Clinic."* Model Cities News Report. (Seattle, WA). 25 March 1970, p. 4.

53. *"Funeral Tomorrow for Powell Barnett, 85".* Seattle Times. 22 March 1971, p. C16.

54. *"Gideon Matthews Gardens Dedication."* The Seattle Medium. 10 Sept. 1986, p. 4b

55. *"He is Short in Size but Long on Service."* Seattle Times. 16 May 1967, p. 1.

56. *"HUD Honors Medgars Pool Design."* Daily Journal of Commerce. (Seattle, WA) 21 Oct.

57. *"Jimi Hendrix Buried After Simple Funeral."* Seattle Times. 2 Oct. 1970, p. A8.

58. *"Local School Named in Honor of Dr. King."* Seattle Medium. 29 Jan. 1974.

59. *"Mass Today for Florentine Ware".* Seattle Times. 21 March 1981, p. B11.

60. *"Memorial to Hendrix is Unveiled."* Seattle Times. 10 June 1983, p. E8.

61. *"Mini Park at 34th and Pike Named Alvin Larkins Park."* Seattle Post Intelligencer. 22 Jan. 1979, p. B1.

62. *"Mr. William Grose: A Puget Sound Pioneer Passes Away."* Seattle Times. 17 July 1898.

63. *"Odessa Brown, Assistant Director CAMP Communication Center."* Central Area Motivation Program Trumpet. July/August 1969, p. 2.

64. *"Panther Leader Charged in Theft."* Seattle Times. 30 July 1968, p. C88.

65. *"Panthers Shed Name and Image."* Seattle Times. 11 Sept. 1977, p. A6.

66. *"Panthers to Open Medical Clinic."* Seattle Post Intelligencer. 25 Nov. 1969, p. 37.

67. *"Park Dedicated to Honor Black Pioneer William Grose."* Seattle Medium. 21 Sept 1983.

68. *"Pratt's Death Shocks Civic Leaders, Friends."* Seattle Post Intelligencer. 27 Jan. 1969.

69. *"Randolph Carter, Head of State Board, Dies."* Seattle Times. 10 Feb. 1970, p. B4.

70. *"Randolph Carter is Named Secretary of Anti-Bias Board."* Seattle Times. 26 Sept. 1963, p. B4.

71. *"Reminiscences of William Gross."* The Seattle Republican. 4 Jan. 1896.

72. *"Rock Theme Chosen for Hendrix Memorial."* Seattle Times. 21 March 1982, p. G13.

73. *"School Name Changed."* Seattle Post Intelligencer. 28 March 1974, p. A10.

74. *"Seattle Leader for Many Years."* Seattle Post Intelligencer. 23 March 1971, p. 42.

75. *"Services Tomorrow for Alvin Larkins, 52."* Seattle Times. 21 May 1977, p. C22.
76. *"Sheriff Calls Pratt's Death 'Assassination'".* Seattle Times. 27 Jan. 1969, p. C88.
77. *"Singer Jimi Hendrix, 27, Dies in London."* Seattle Post Intelligencer. 19 Sept. 1970, p. 9.
78. *"Struggling for Social Justice."* Seattle Post Intelligencer. 30 Aug. 1976, p. A8.
79. *"YWCA Names New Executive."* Seattle Post Intelligencer. 22 Aug. 1965, p6W.
80. *"Y.W.C.A. to Hold Reception Honoring Two New Officials."* Seattle Times. 2 Aug. 1965, p. 12S.

Interviews

81. Otis Bean 1983
82. Mr. and Mrs. Oscar Braxton 1983
83. Toby Burton 1995
84. Emilie Capps 1983
85. Luther Carr 1996
86. Mrs. Randolph Carter 1980
87. John Cannon 1980
88. Elmer Dixon 1995
89. Isadora Downs 1992
90. Danie Eagleton 1996
91. Lillian Gideon 1996
92. Judge Charles Johnson 1980
93. Ginny Larkins 1983
94. Alvirita Little 1995
95. De Charlene Williams 1983

Manuscripts, Brochures and Unpublished Materials

96. Powell R. Barnett Papers. University of Washington Libraries.
97. Odessa Brown Children's Clinic. Fact Sheet. 1994.
98. Catholic Community Services brochure. 1991.
99. Elmer Dixon. History of Carolyn Downs Family Medical Center. 1989.
100. William H. Dixon Papers. University of Washington Libraries.
101. Carolyn Downs Family Medical Center brochure. 1995.
102. East Madison YMCA. Dedication Program. 1965.
103. East Madison YMCA. History.
104. Russell Gideon Funeral Program. 1985.
105. Hayes, Ralph. Bridging Generations; A Tribute to Black History. National Council of Negro Women. 1981.
106. King County Landmarks and Heritage Commission, Office of Cultural Resources. Dr. Martin Luther King, Jr. Historical Paper #10. 1996.
107. Martin Luther King, Jr. Memorial Committee. Renewing the Dream. 1989.

108. Dr. Martin Luther King, Jr. Historical Paper No. 10. King County Historic
Preservation Program, King County Cultural Resources Division. 1996.
109. Pratt Fine Arts Center Brochure. 1996.
110. Seattle Housing Authority. Annual Report. 1995.
111. Seattle Parks and Recreation. Board Minutes. December 4, 1969.
112. Seattle Parks and Recreation. Board Minutes. October 7, 1976.
113. Seattle Parks and Recreation. News Release. August 31, 1982.
114. Seattle Parks and Recreation. News Release. November 10, 1982.
115. Seattle Public Library. Douglass Truth Community Study. 1984.
116. Seattle School District. Board Policies. 1972.
117. Seattle School District. Board Minutes. March 27, 1974.
118. Seattle School District. Board Minutes. February 7, 1996.
119. Seattle School District. Board Minutes. February 21, 1996.
120. Seattle School District. Board Minutes. March 20, 1996.
121. Don Sherwood files. Archives of the City of Seattle.
122. Flo Ware Funeral Program. 1981.
123. Wilcox, Shirley. Alpha Kappa Alpha Library Project.

ONE OF THE MOST IMPORTANT ways we build community identity and pride is to remember those who have touched our lives and who have inspired us to greater things by their example. Many of our fundamental rights, and things we take for granted, were gained for us through the struggle and sacrifice of others. We are—all of us—the inheritors and stewards of the legacy provided for us by those who have gone before.

Parks, buildings and landscapes are often named in honor of our elders, as a reminder that the job of protecting our rights and of preserving and passing on their precious legacy is never finished. Remembering the trailblazers who have shown us the way helps us in "bridging the generations" and in sharing our values with others.

In this guide, Mary Henry has provided us with an eloquent means for remembering the courage, the genius and the sacrifices of those whose legacy continues to enrich our lives and our communities.

Charles Payton
King County Landmarks and Heritage Program